# THE TENTH: 7 STEPS TO TAKING BACK CONTROL OF YOUR MONEY AND BEING A FAITHFUL STEWARD

ISBN 978-1-958751-12-1 (paperback)

Printed in the United States of America

# *Table of Contents*

Table of Contents ------------------------------------------------------- 3

Introduction ------------------------------------------------------------ 4

Chapter One: The Duality of Stewardship ----------------------------- 7

Chapter Two: The Positive Privilege of Tithing – An Old

Testament View----------------------------------------------------------- 10

Chapter Three: God's Promise to the Tither------------------------ 15

Chapter Four: The Positive Privilege of Tithing-A New Testament

View--------------------------------------------------------------------- 20

Chapter Five: It's Okay to Be Wealthy-------------------------------- 24

Chapter Six: 7 Steps to Taking Back Control of Your Money --- 28

Chapter Seven: Greed and Debt -------------------------------------- 50

Chapter Eight: Financial Attitude ------------------------------------ 54

Chapter Nine: The Final Point-Saving ------------------------------- 58

In Closing --------------------------------------------------------------- 62

A Tithing Bibliography ------------------------------------------------- 64

# *The Tenth: 7 Steps to Taking Back Control of Your Money and Being a Faithful Steward*

# *Introduction*

Have you ever noticed how it always seems to be the "season for giving"?  Giving to the church for stewardship; giving gifts for Christmas; giving thanks on Thanksgiving; giving presents for birthdays, anniversaries, showers, and all those other "special" occasions.  With all this giving, did you ever wonder where the money tree is so you could afford all this giving?  Through this book, I thought I would offer some suggestions and commentary on how we look at giving (stewardship/tithing) and ways to make it affordable (financial planning).  To help accomplish this task I'll be drawing on my experience as a stewardship leader for the past twenty plus years and other resources I

have gleaned from my journey of learning to be a good and faithful servant to all that the Lord as entrusted to me to steward as well.

To begin, we should look at what stewardship means to us. Is it filling out a pledge card each Fall? Or writing a check each week? Or returning to God a portion of what He has first given to us? *Or*, does stewardship challenge us to assume the posture of one who serves. To serve God first because He has already given to us first as II Chronicles 29:11-16 shows us how God has already given first. To serve our neighbor as Luke 10:29-37 shows us. To serve ourselves by being good stewards with what God has given to us. It does not matter so much what we have, but what we do with it that makes all the difference in the world. This is reflected in II Corinthians 8:11-12, "Having started the ball rolling so enthusiastically, you should carry this project through to completion just as gladly, giving whatever you can out of whatever you have. Let your enthusiastic idea at the start be equaled by realistic action now. If you are really eager to give, then it isn't important how much you have to give. God wants you to give what you have, not what you haven't" (TLB).

If we accept the challenge of stewardship and assume the posture of one who serves, then it invites us to practice generosity with thankful hearts and encompasses our whole being, not just sharing our possessions.

To begin, let us look at the Duality of Stewardship.

# *Chapter One: The Duality of Stewardship*

In the introduction we looked at what stewardship means, the challenge of assuming the posture of one who serves. With some inspiration from David Hinze's book *To Give and Give Again*, here we look at the Duality of Stewardship.

Stewardship is what we do with what creation gives to us. It is the acquisition, accumulation and management of gifts. However, it is more: stewardship is the sharing, giving and release of resources. It invites us to practice generosity with thankful hearts. Where we know only gathering and keeping, it teaches us that we are out of step with creation, that creation is harmonized by the cyclic rhythm of receiving **and** giving, the alternation of having and yielding.

Wealth and comfort are not readily compatible with spiritual vitality unless they are coupled with strong impulses for generosity, service and uncommon sharing. In our time and place of superabundance, when we know the price of everything but the value of little, the relationship of people and communities to their goods and possessions is central to any faith expression. Having much but giving little is an offense to the pursuit and practice of Christianity, especially in the face of the coexistent presence of enormous wealth and gross poverty in our own country and around the world. The Spirit yearns for those who have to respond to those who have not.  In a Hasidic story, the wife of the Rabbi of Roptchitz says to him, "your prayer was lengthy today. Have you succeeded in bringing it about that the rich should be more generous in their gifts to the poor?"  The Rabbi replies, "Half of my prayer I have accomplished.  The poor are willing to accept them".  The human spirit suffers in the disparities between rich and poor.

The apostle Paul wrote, "If I speak in the tongues of mortals and of angles, but do not have love [caritas, charity or love in action], I am a noisy gong or a clanging cymbal" (I Cor. 13:1, NRS. Translation added.).  And the poet John Donne preached, "This only charity, to do all, all that we can".  Because we have not understood the necessity of living with thankful and generous hearts, we are less than whole people, unfulfilled in our spiritual yearning and disquieted within despite our general prosperity and affluence.  The outward acts of generous giving and service are the key to inner peace and the meaning of life.  This is stewardship of life, and, it is living in imitation of Christ as scripture enjoins us.

# Chapter Two: The Positive Privilege of Tithing – An Old Testament View

Throughout life, it has been observed that some people struggle with the concept of tithing.  Usually, the only reason people ever struggle over tithing is simply because they do not completely understand the concept.  Tithe means one tenth.  Our numeric system is based on groups of ten; ten is actually as high as anyone needs count, as all other numbers are repetitions of the same.  When we give God ten percent, we are symbolically saying that all that I have belongs to You.  It is the highest honor, as it is the highest number we can reach without repetition.  Tithing is devoting the first tenth of your income to God and His Kingdom.  Look at Leviticus 27:30-33, "All tithes from the land, whether the seed from the ground or the fruit from the tree, are the LORD's; they are holy to the LORD.  If persons wish to redeem any of their tithes, they must add one-fifth to them.  All tithes of herd and flock, every tenth one that passes under the shepherd's staff, shall be holy to the LORD. Let no one inquire whether it is good or bad, or make substitution for it; if one makes substitution for it, then both it and the substitute shall be holy and cannot be redeemed" (NRS).  Look at what the word of the Lord says- that tithing *begins* at 10%.  Not that we should work up 10% as if it where some kind of goal to achieve.  Moreover, that if we do not begin at 10%, we want to redeem part of what God commands, and then He wants a fifth or 20% added to it.  In banker's terms, that's a 20% interest rate on the loan we are taking from God.

We do not tithe just because it is written in the Law that you must tithe, even though that is not a bad reason. However, tithing the first fruits of our income has always been part of God's economic plan, long before the Law was ever handed down to Moses.  Melchizedek, the king of Salem, was also a priest of the most high God (Genesis 14 and Hebrews 7).  Abraham paid tithe to that high priest in approximately 1883 B.C. – over 425 years *before* the Law was ever given to Moses.  That 4,000-year-old example is to be followed by us today as we give our gifts to God, of whom the Scriptures declare: You are a priest forever, according to the order of Melchizedek (Heb 7:17, NRS).

Jacob, when confronted by God in his "ladder-day" experience at Bethel, vowed two things to God: (1) I will choose Yahweh as my God. (2) I will give you back a tenth of everything you give me. (Gen. 28:21-22, NRS).

When it became necessary for the Law to be written down, God certainly never overlooked the beautiful concept of tithing.

"You must tithe all of your crops every year. Bring this tithe to eat before the Lord your God at the place he shall choose as his sanctuary; this applies to your tithes of grain, new wine, olive oil, and the firstborn of your flocks and herds. The purpose of tithing is to teach you always to put God first in your lives" (Deut. 14:22-23, TLB).  God does not need your tithe; after all, He created and blessed us with all that we have. He uses the tithe to teach us principles and obedience to the word of God. It is an expression of our sacrifice and worship to Him. The tithe proves our creditability of faith. We may say we are disciples of Christ with our tongues but if we do not have discipline in our finances by putting God first and obeying his command to render Him his tenth, how can our words ring true? Remember our description of stewardship from the introduction? Assuming the posture of one who serves. How can we truly be in service to God if we are picking and choosing which commands to be obedient to? Paying Him should be a priority above all else. Are you paying God what is right or are you giving God what is left? When we give the tithe, we not only honor God but we let Him know that our commitment to His work is greater than our commitment to money.

Every place God commands tithing He balances it by promising that if you put Him first, He will see to it that your needs will be met by His sufficiency! Solomon attested to that principle nearly 500 years after the Law was written.

"Honour the Lord with your wealth as the first charge on all your earnings; then your granaries will be filled with corn and your vats bursting with new wine (Prov. 3:9-10, NEB)."

"In everything you do, put God first and He will direct you and crown your efforts with success (Prov. 3:6, TLB)."

Less than 400 years before Christ was born, the Hebrew people had forgotten God's commands.  To put it plainly, they had made an absolute mess out of their lives and their nation.  They had changed.  But the prophet Malachi appeared to remind them that God does not change:  before the Law, in the Law, or after the Law.

"No; I, Yahweh, do not change; and you have not ceased to be children of Jacob! Ever since the days of your ancestors, you have evaded my statutes and not observed them. Return to me and I will return to you, says Yahweh Sabaoth. You ask, 'How are we to return? Can a human being cheat God?' Yet you try to cheat me! You ask, 'How do we try to cheat you?' Over tithes and contributions. A curse lies on you because you, this whole nation, try to cheat me. Bring the tithes in full to the treasury, so that there is food in my house; put me to the test now like this, says Yahweh Sabaoth, and see if I do not open the floodgates of heaven for you and pour out an abundant blessing for you. For your sakes, I shall forbid the locust to destroy the produce of your soil or prevent the vine from bearing fruit in your field, says Yahweh Sabaoth, and all the nations will call you blessed, for you will be a land of delights, says Yahweh Sabaoth" (Mal. 3:6-12, NJB).

In the next chapter we will take a closer look at this passage, as it reveals God's promises to the tither.

# Chapter Three: God's Promise to the Tither

In the last chapter we discussed the Old Testament view of tithing and ended with the passage from Malachi 3:6-12 that reveals God's will towards a tither. This time we will take a closer look at this passage, as it reveals five "I will" promises and a challenge from God. Let us begin at Malachi 3:10, "Bring the tithes in **full** to the treasury, so that there is food in my house; put me to the test now like this, says Yahweh Sabaoth, and see if I do not open the floodgates of heaven for you and pour out an abundant blessing for you (singular)." (emphasis/comment added)(NJB). Or in the New English Bible, "Bring the tithes into the treasury, **all of them**, let there be food in my house. Put me to the proof, says the Lord of Hosts, and see if I do not open the windows in the sky and pour *a* blessing on you as long as there is need" (emphasis added). Within this verse are our first two "I will" promises and God's challenge.

First, He says I will open the floodgates or windows of heaven to the tither. That is quite a powerful image! Close your eyes; picture yourself looking over either the Hoover or Glen Canyon Dam. See all that water being held back by the dam. Acres and acres of life giving water held in place by a single immoveable structure. Now, the floodgates to those dams are opened, fully opened. Feel the power, hear the thunder, and see the force as megatons of water explode from those floodgates! Now, imagine that is the blessing God is releasing to you because of your tithe. A blessing in abundance that is yours as long as there is a need! And this leads straight into the second "I will" promise. God is releasing *a* blessing, singular.  Imagine having *a* blessing that is like the power of water released from a floodgate.  A single blessing!  There are examples all around us of this promise.  Colonel Sanders, a tither, received a single blessing of being able to cook great chicken.  He has been gone now over 20 years and his blessing is still pouring forth.  Ted Geisel, Dr. Seuss, had a blessing of being able to write children's stories.  Next time you are in the library, just look at all the different categories of books there are to choose from and remind yourself Dr. Seuss had *a* blessing.  Consider Bill Gates.  He was blessed with writing a single software program for IBM, the Disk Operating System, DOS.  Look what became of that single blessing.

Look closely at this verse, see the words "see if I do not" or "Put me to the proof".  This is God's challenge to us regarding tithing.  He is asking us to challenge His will on the subject of tithing.  That is quite a powerful challenge.  In contemporary language, He is "calling us out", drawing a line in the sand, asking us to try to prove His words and will false.  Simply put He is saying, "I dare you to tithe and see if I don't give you what I said I would give you.  Prove me a liar"!  Tithing must be extremely important if God, the Supreme Commander of all Forces, the CEO of, well, of Everything, the Creator of Heaven and Earth, is willing to stake His reputation on it.

The next two "I will" promises are found in Malachi 3:11. Again, I will use both the New English Bible and The Jerusalem Bible for the translations.  "I will forbid pests to destroy the produce of your soil or make your vines barren" (NEB). "For your sakes, I shall forbid the locust to destroy the produce of your soil or prevent the vine from bearing fruit in your field" (NJB). In this verse, the crops are representative of our blessing received from God. The pests or locust represents those forces that are preventing us from tithing and receiving God's "floodgate" blessing. Those forces could be internal and represent our own weakness and limitations such as, "I never seem to have enough money to tithe" (limitation-lack of budgeting education), or "I don't know where my money goes, all I know is that I never have enough" (weakness-impulse buying). Or they could be external and represent our enemies or even the Devil, such as "as soon as my credit cards are paid off, then I'll have enough to begin tithing" (enemies), or "when I can stop paying for my kids school activities, then I'll have the extra money to tithe" (Devil). Remember, one of the benefits of tithing is that it teaches us to put God first and allow Him to vanquish these pests. The forth "I will" promise is centered on the concept of not letting our vines become barren. In other words, letting our blessing come to full fruition and not having premature delivery of it. In this "I will" God is promising the tither He will teach us how to hold onto our blessing and use it at the appropriate time.

The fifth "I will" promise is found in Malachi 3:12, "All nations shall count you happy, for yours shall be a favored land," (NEB). "all the nations will call you blessed, for you will be a land of delights," (NJB). In this promise, God is saying He will favor and bless the tither. What does it mean to be "favored"? Synonyms for the word favor included chosen, esteem, preferential. Therefore, by tithing God will give preferentially to us. He will esteem us. He will include us has His chosen. Could this not also mean He is willing to view us as His "favored" sons and daughters? To not only receive the preferential treatment of a favored child, but also avoid punishment and have our mistakes overlooked. What a wonderful blessing to receive from tithing, to have God declare us as favored and to live our lives in delight and happy!

In our next chapter we will take a New Testament view of the positive privilege of tithing.

# Chapter Four: The Positive Privilege of Tithing-A New Testament View

In the previous chapters we observed the Old Testament view of tithing, the Law, and took a close examination of some key verses in Malachi. This time we observe the New Testament perspective of tithing through Christ. He came not to destroy any Law, but to fulfill it. He declared that "Yes, you should tithe". It is a good place start…but a tragic place to quit.

"Yes, woe upon you, Pharisees, and you other religious leaders-hypocrites! For you tithe down to the last mint leaf in your gardens, but ignore the important things-justice and mercy and faith. Yes, you should tithe, but you shouldn't leave the more important things undone" (Mt. 23:23, TLB).

While proclaiming nothing that would in any way weaken the position of the Law on tithing, Christ went on to teach a more excellent way, a way of making available to God 100 percent of everything you own in an attitude and act of complete commitment.

"As he stood in the Temple, he was watching the rich tossing their gifts into the collection box. Then a poor widow came by and dropped in two small copper coins. Really, he remarked, this poor widow has given more than all the rest of them combined. For they have given little of what they didn't need, but she, poor as she is, had given everything she has" (Lk. 21:1-4, TLB).

Christ knew that "tithing…plus…" must become a way of life. He taught that the failure to give all is simply a failure to understand God's character, but in giving all, the very character of God is developed in the giver. "Anyone who takes care of a little child like this is caring for me! And whoever cares for me is caring for God who sent me. Your care for others is the measure of your greatness" (Lk. 9:48, TLB).

Today, tithing is simply your testimony to God's total ownership. It is an external evidence of an internal commitment, an outward expression of inward attitude. Tithing is not a heavenly insurance policy against hassle or persecution; but when given as a testimony, always reaps great dividends because God is then able to take direct control over that which He owns anyway and multiply it accordingly.

We should give the tithe willing and happily. "Remember this: Whoever sows sparingly will also reap sparingly, and whoever sows generously will also reap generously. Each man should give what he has decided in his heart to give, not reluctantly or under compulsion, for God loves a cheerful giver" (II Cor. 9:6-7, NIV). God doesn't want us to have the attitude that we are cutting a deal with Him or paying off the church. God wants gifts given out of a heart of gratitude, obedience and trust. A generous heart will not flinch at the idea of tithing and will always find that it gives way beyond the ten percent. This type of generosity protects us from falling prey to the sin of serving money. We are not to serve money. Money is to serve us, and we should serve God by using is according to His plan.

"It is possible to give away and become richer! It is also possible to hold on too tightly and lose everything. Yes, the liberal man shall be rich! By watering others, he waters himself" (Prov. 11:24-25, TLB).

The purpose then of tithing, as we learned from Deuteronomy 14, "is to teach you always to put God first in your lives". It is a privilege to be able to tithe.

Now you may be declaring to yourself, "Yes, this is all well and good. I agree. I should be giving at least 10% to church. But who's going to tell my creditors I can't afford to pay them their due and how will I ever make ends meet if I commit to giving 10%"! The next chapters will focus on how we can tame our debt, control our finances and be able to give our proper tithe to church. Consider it your training for meeting the challenge of the parable of the talents (Mt. 25:14-30, Lk. 19:11-26).

# *Chapter Five: It's Okay to Be Wealthy*

Now that we have a biblical foundation on why we should tithe, how do we establish a good foundation on how to tithe? How do we find the money to tithe and meet all the other financial obligations we have? The short answer is the accumulation of wealth. Let me just say up front that the accumulation of wealth should never be our final goal. Wealth in the Kingdom is not the end, but the means to the end. The end is that the gospel will be preached to the entire world and broken lives will be redeemed and restored. Ultimately, God should be our financial advisor. Just like the supply of manna given to the Israelites in the wilderness, so will be our financial supply. If we take what He gives and use it as He commands, the supply will continue. If we are generous, God will continue to be generous to us. Nevertheless, if, like the Israelites, we hoard our supply, we will find that in time it will dry up. Remember the parable of the talents. To those that increased their original pounds, much was given. To the one that did nothing, even what was given to him was taken away.

Since we will also be discussing money, I would like to make it clear that money in itself in neither evil nor good. It is what you do with it that colors it with moral relativity. Money simply makes you more of what you already were before you had it. If you were a giver before you had money, you will still be generous once you have wealth. Money shows your values and preferences. If I want to know whom you really are; all I need to do is look at your spending habits.  What you do with your money shows me what you love and value.

If we are to pursue wealth, we must have the right attitude towards it.  I Timothy 6:6-9 states, "They think religion should yield dividends; and of course religion does yield high dividends, but only to the man whose resources are within.  We brought nothing into the world; for that matter we cannot take anything with us when we leave, but if we have food and covering, we may rest content.  Those who want to be rich fall into temptations and snares and many foolish harmful desires which plunge men into ruin and perdition" (NEB).  Verse 6 teaches us that godliness coupled with contentment is great gain.  The word gain means profit.  A profit is what is accrued when the transactions is over.  When all is said and done, you want to profit from every stage and age of your life.  Profit comes when the faithful are contented, not being led by the lust of success nor driven by the promise of wealth, but calmly assured that God knows the whens, the whos and the hows of blessing His people.  Verse 7 assures us that nothing tangible is eternal.  No matter what we have attained, none of it is transportable to where we are going. The things seen are temporal, the things not seen are eternal, and never the twain shall meet.  Verse 8 makes the distinction between needs and wants.  This allows the indigenous person who lives in a hut in India to say, "Thank you, Lord," just like the mansion dweller in Hollywood.  They both thank God for the basics of life.  We cannot want to say "thank you" until we have attained the latest and newest definition of success. It is wrong not to thank God for where we are and what we have right now. It blocks the floodgate of future blessing with unthankfulness. Verse 9 does not speak against being rich. It speaks against the desire to be rich. Being rich is not the goal. If it is, it becomes the god we worship, and the methods by which we attain it will take us farther from the true God who freely gives us all things.

Our first step toward the wealth that will gain us our tithe is establishing a budget. A budget is not to restrict us from enjoying life but it is a tool to help us focus our finances on those goals that will allow us to lead a fulfilling life.

Next chapter, seven steps to taking back control of your money and being a faithful steward.

# *Chapter Six: 7 Steps to Taking Back Control of Your Money*

Any budget will work if you follow it.  So why don't they work?  "It's just too complicated".  "It's just too much trouble".  "It' just never seems to work".  Why?  Because we overspend, we blow it, we mess it up, and we fail.

This budget system allows for occasional lapses in financial reasoning and it is simple to set up and use.  As for being too much trouble, well, very few things are truly worthwhile that are not some trouble.  This budget is very little trouble...really.  If you follow this monthly management system, you will

- Know where your money goes.
- Have full control over your spending.
- Never blow your budget because it can be easily fixed.

## *Step 1-Commitment*

Questions to ask yourself about taking care of the money you earn.

*Do I want to be responsible for taking care of all my money all the time?*

____ YES, YES, YES

____ I don't know, what do I have to give up?

____ It sounds like too much work!

____ I have tried it.  It was not much fun.

*Where are you now with your money?*

____ I take care of all of my money all of the time.

____ I take care of most of my money most of the time.

____ I take care of some of my money some of the time.

____ I haven't the foggiest idea what you are talking about!

____ I manage somehow!

*I would like to:*

____ Pay off all of my credit cards and live totally on cash.

____ Pay off my car loan early.

____ Pay off my mortgage early and avoid thousands of dollars in interest.

____ Pay off all my loans early.

**If all my loans were paid off, I would have $_____ extra each month!!**

## *Step 2-Determine the Importance of Money in Your life*

Most people feel money is important to them but not everyone takes care of it as though it is. Answer the following questions to determine how you really do take care of your money. Don't worry if you answer "No" or "Sometimes" to some of these. Now you will know the areas that need attention to make your money work for you.

I keep accurate records:

> Yes     No     Sometimes

I keep my records organized:

> Yes     No     Sometimes

I plan my purchases in advance:

> Yes     No     Sometimes

I do not buy on impulse:

> Yes     No     Sometimes

I have a budget/spending plan:

> Yes     No     Sometimes

I have specific financial goals:

       Yes     No     Sometimes

I save money regularly:

       Yes     No     Sometimes

I know exactly where my money is going:

       Yes     No     Sometimes

I pay off my credit cards monthly:

      · Yes     No     Sometimes

I feel "in control" of my money:

       Yes     No     Sometimes

I reconcile my bank statement every month:

       Yes     No     Sometimes

I do not overdraw my checking account:

       Yes     No     Sometimes

I keep accurate records of all ATM transactions:

       Yes     No     Sometimes

I have auto insurance:

     Yes     No     Sometimes

I have disability insurance:

     Yes     No     Sometimes

## *Step 3-Know Exactly How Much Money You Make Each Month. Don't Estimate!*

If you are paid only once a month and have one income, this is fairly cut and dry. If you have a two-income family, for instance, you often work overtime, and your spouse has a second job, it can get complicated.

Remember *gross income* is before tax and *net income* is take home pay.

| | |
|---|---|
| Net income per month (self) | $_____ |
| Net income per month (spouse) | $_____ |
| Overtime per month (self) | $_____ |
| Overtime per month (spouse) | $_____ |
| Other income per month | $_____ |
| **Total family take home pay per month** | $_____ |

## Step 4-Find Out How Much You Spend and On What

Now this probably looks like any old budget form you have seen-BUT IT ISN'T!  The reason most budgets don't work is that you don't really know how much you spend each month.  So, first write down what you think you spend in column 1.  Then look at your tracking sheet to really know for sure how much you spend and write it down in column 2.  However, don't put any figures in the #2 column until you use the tracking sheet for a least a month (except for fixed expenses, they don't change).  The third column is actually only the first half of your new budget.  The next worksheet will tell you the rest.

| | Column 1<br>How much do I think I spend | Column 2<br>After tracking my expenses, this is exactly what I spend | Column 3<br>This is my new spending plan (budget) |
|---|---|---|---|
| **Fixed Expenses** | | | |
| Rent/Mortgage | | | |
| Second Mortgage | | | |
| Car Payment/Lease | | | |
| Lot Rent/Association Dues | | | |
| Student Loans | | | |
| Alimony/Child Support | | | |
| Child Care | | | |
| Medical Insurance | | | |

| | | | |
|---|---|---|---|
| Life Insurance | | | |
| Homeowners/Renter Insurance | | | |
| Monthly Medical Bills | | | |
| Cable TV | | | |
| Savings | | | |
| Tithing | | | |
| Other Fixed Expense: | | | |
| Other Fixed Expense: | | | |
| Other Fixed Expense: | | | |
| TOTAL FIXED EXPENSES | | | |
| **Flexible Expenses** | | | |
| Electricity/Gas | | | |
| Telephone | | | |
| Water/Trash | | | |
| Groceries | | | |
| Food at work | | | |
| Dining Out | | | |
| School Lunches | | | |
| Gasoline | | | |
| Bus, Car Pool, Parking | | | |
| Personal items | | | |
| Laundry/Dry Cleaning | | | |
| Hair Care | | | |
| Newspapers/Magazines | | | |
| Children's Allowance | | | |
| Occasional Baby-sitting | | | |
| Recreation | | | |
| Donations | | | |
| Postage | | | |
| Pet Expenses | | | |

| | | | |
|---|---|---|---|
| Lessons/Memberships | | | |
| Other Flexible Expenses: | | | |
| Other Flexible Expenses: | | | |
| Other Flexible Expenses: | | | |
| TOTAL FLEXIBLE EXPENSES | | | |
| **Non-Monthly Expenses** | | | |
| Car Repair/Maintenance | | | |
| Prescriptions | | | |
| Clothing | | | |
| Car Insurance | | | |
| Doctor/Dentist | | | |
| Licenses/Taxes | | | |
| Home Repair/Furnishing | | | |
| TOTAL NON-MONTHLY EXPENSES | | | |
| | | | |
| **Debt & Credit Expenses** | | | |
| Credit Cards: | Monthly Payment | N/A | This is what I would like to pay |
| 1. | | | |
| 2. | | | |
| 3. | | | |
| 4. | | | |
| 5. | | | |
| 6. | | | |
| 7. | | | |
| 8. | | | |
| **Other Loans** | | | |
| 1. | | | |

| | | | |
|---|---|---|---|
| 2. | | | |
| 3. | | | |

TOTAL MONTHLY EXPENSES =   $_____

TOTAL MONTHLY INCOME =    $_____

VERDICT (plus or minus)     $_____

When completing this worksheet here are some helpful hints to remember:

Fixed expenses remain the same each month. There should be no surprises. These expenses do not need to be accounted for on your tracking worksheet

Flexible expenses are trouble waiting to happen. Tracking these will plug up holes in your wallet. Some of the worst troublemakers are food (all food), eating out, recreation and personal items (you know, like going to the drug store for shampoo and coming out with two big sacks of ???).

Non-monthly expenses can be deadly to budgets because we often don't put money aside for these (the, oh my gosh, my twice a year car insurance payment is due tomorrow and there is not money to pay it, problem). These expenses need to be tracked. In the meantime, try to determine what you have spent on these during the last 12 months, divide by 12 and enter that amount. It probably won't be accurate now but do your best.

Don't forget about your credit cards. The column that reads "This is what I would like to pay" is there because paying more is obviously going to get the debts paid faster. After tracking your expenses, you might "find" extra cash to throw at these debts.

## Step 5-Tracking, The Secret to a Happy Life

All right, maybe tracking isn't exactly the most important ingredient to a happy life, but at least it got your attention! Besides, tracking your money daily **can**:

- Help "find" extra money.
- Plug up spending leaks.
- Give you control of one aspect of your life.

Now you are probably wondering what is meant by "finding" money. Well, many of us spend money unconsciously almost every day...a little here, a little there, and who remembers? And exactly how much did you spend on "eating out" last month? You say you only "eat out" once a month and you know exactly what you spend. Well, maybe, but what about the lunches you "eat out" at work, the corn dog and soda you have at the mall, the fast-food stops as you are rushing to an evening meeting after work, the trips to the vending machine at work for a soda and candy bar? What about all of that? *Now* are you sure?

You can be and it will be so satisfying!  When you see how much you actually spend on certain flexible categories, you might decide *that* money could be better used.  Found money!

Here's how the following chart works to help you track your daily expenses:

1.  Determine the categories to be tracked ( basically, all flexible and non-monthly expense) and enter them at the top of the chart.
2.  *Every day*, list every dollar spent.
3.  To remember what we spend each and every day is difficult, but there is a very easy tool to help, receipts.  Just stuff the receipts in your wallet as you go about your day.  In the evening, dump out the receipts and enter that day's damage.  The only problem with receipts is vending machines don't give receipts.  So, keep a small piece of paper in your wallet and record each amount.

That is all there is to it.  It takes five minutes a day.  At the end of the month, add up the columns.  You are now in control of your money.  One hint: do not stick this chart in a drawer. You won't use it.  Put it on the refrigerator so it will be "in your face" every day.  You may also want to make copies of this tracking sheet for every new month.

| Your Tracking Worksheet | | | | | | | |
|---|---|---|---|---|---|---|---|
| Date | | | | | | | |
| 1 | | | | | | | |
| 2 | | | | | | | |
| 3 | | | | | | | |
| 4 | | | | | | | |
| 5 | | | | | | | |
| 6 | | | | | | | |
| 7 | | | | | | | |
| 8 | | | | | | | |
| 9 | | | | | | | |
| 10 | | | | | | | |
| 11 | | | | | | | |
| 12 | | | | | | | |
| 13 | | | | | | | |
| 14 | | | | | | | |
| 15 | | | | | | | |
| 16 | | | | | | | |
| 17 | | | | | | | |
| 18 | | | | | | | |
| 19 | | | | | | | |
| 20 | | | | | | | |
| 21 | | | | | | | |
| 22 | | | | | | | |
| 23 | | | | | | | |
| 24 | | | | | | | |
| 25 | | | | | | | |
| 26 | | | | | | | |
| 27 | | | | | | | |
| 28 | | | | | | | |

| | | | | | | | |
|---|---|---|---|---|---|---|---|
| **29** | | | | | | | |
| **30** | | | | | | | |
| **31** | | | | | | | |
| **Totals** | | | | | | | |
| **Expense Plan** | | | | | | | |
| **Over/Under Budget** | | | | | | | |

## Step 6-Create Your New Spending Plan

This is the worksheet that is going to make you a star at budgeting.  It is going to change you from "budget challenged" to a money saving, big success!  Yes, perhaps there is a bit of over-selling this method, but sometimes it is necessary to pretty up this somewhat dull but very important material to get you interested.

Here is how the budget worksheet actually works:

1.  After completing Step 4 and Step 5, enter every category that applies to you.  Under the Budget/Date Column, enter your new amounts and if it is a bill to be paid by a certain date, enter the date due.
2.  Enter the amount of each of your family's paychecks.  The fun begins now!  From this point, use a pencil because you'll be erasing a lot.
3.  Determine when the bills need to be paid and figure out from which check each bill needs to be taken.  If the entire amount of a single bill cannot be taken from just one check, highlight it or use a colored pen (see the example worksheet).

## Example Budget Worksheet

| | BUDGET | DATE | 1ST CHECK: $425 | 2ND CHECK: $425 | 3RD CHECK: $425 | 4th CHECK $425 |
|---|---|---|---|---|---|---|
| Rent | 450 | 1st | 225 | | | 225 |
| Electric & Gas | 100 | 10th | | 100 | | |
| Phone | 40 | 10th | | 40 | | |
| Cable | 25 | 10th | | 25 | | |
| Car payment | 125 | 1st | 125 | | | |
| Child care | 225 | 30th | | 75 | 75 | 75 |
| Car insurance | 50 | 30th | | | 50 | |
| Groceries | 220 | | 55 | 55 | 55 | 55 |
| Gas | 60 | | 15 | 15 | 15 | 15 |
| Clothes | 50 | | | | 50 | |
| Car repair | 25 | | | | | 25 |
| Allowance | 50 | | | 25 | 25 | |
| Entertainment | 40 | | | | 40 | |
| Dry cleaning | 10 | | | 10 | | |
| Tithing | 30 | | | | | 30 |
| Household | 25 | | | | 25 | |

| | | | | | | |
|---|---|---|---|---|---|---|
| Prescriptions | 10 | | | | 10 | |
| Savings | 80 | | | | 80 | |
| Visa | 25 | 10$^{th}$ | | 25 | | |
| Macy's | 50 | 10$^{th}$ | | 50 | | |
| Totals | 1690 | | 420 | 420 | 425 | 425 |

As you can see from the example worksheet, you'll know exactly when there will be enough money to pay each bill and when money is available for various expenses. The beauty of this worksheet is that you are able to truly see the budget working day by day, week by week. Do you want to buy shoes this month? By looking at the worksheet, you know you can't buy them until whatever check is allocated for clothes, for example. Another good feature of this worksheet is the ability to note a shortage or overage. You will want to make copies of your completed worksheet so a fresh one can be placed on your refrigerator each month to make notations.

## *BUDGET WORKSHEET*

| | BUDGET | DATE | 1ST CHECK $ | 2ND CHECK $ | 3RD CHECK $ | 4th CHECK $ |
|---|---|---|---|---|---|---|
| | | | | | | |
| | | | | | | |
| | | | | | | |
| | | | | | | |
| | | | | | | |
| | | | | | | |
| | | | | | | |
| | | | | | | |
| | | | | | | |
| | | | | | | |
| | | | | | | |
| | | | | | | |
| | | | | | | |
| Totals | | | | | | |

## Step 7-Planning for Major Purchases

Aren't you getting excited?  Are there beginning to be visions of perfectly balanced months dancing in your head?  Can't you just see your budget worksheet glowing with good health and current, accurate figures, every time you look at it?

There is one more step, however, that will make it even more perfect:  The Major Purchases Planning List. You know what these are; the trips, holidays and other big things we don't plan for very well.  You often put these items on your credit cards!

Planning for them and figuring how to pay for them will keep you from using credit cards or dipping into savings, meant for emergencies.   Using the example below, let's see how you can work these major purchases into the Budget Worksheet.

| Description | December 2020 | June 2021 | August 2021 |
|---|---|---|---|
| Christmas | $300 | | |
| Sister's Wedding | | $200 | |
| Vacation | | | $400 |

You know these expenses are coming up in the next several months.  Let's figure out how to pay for them or if you will have to make some adjustments.

Look at our example Budget Worksheet.  Do you see any of these categories listed?  Nope!  Major budget snafu here!  Let's see how to fix it.

**Christmas:** Let family members know of your new spending plan without credit cards.  Be creative-give gifts of your time or craft projects that you made.  Limit spending to $100 for Christmas.

**Sister's Wedding:**  Your share of the shower expense will be $50.00 and the rest ($150) is for a gift.  A lovely gift can be purchased for $100, so we reduced the wedding expense to $150.

**Vacation:** Cutting the vacation budget in half ($200) until your spending in under control would be the best alternative.

So, the major purchases for the next several months have been cut in half, from $900 to $450, but they are still not in the budget.  At least, however, you only have to find $38 per month extra instead of $75 per month!

By having the Budget Worksheet, it is much easier to see where it will come from and to make sure it will be taken out.  You may not agree with this example of cost cutting and you would obviously determine your own priorities when developing your budget. Don't forget that once you have determined your major purchases cost to go back and add then to your budget.

Well there you have it, your new spending plan. It works, it is easy, it is effective and it is adaptable to change. You will be in control at long last. Life is good.

Now I know, literally tackling your finances is a fearful and daunting task. It is a major challenge to change your money habits and to truly put God first by tithing. By giving 10% of your gross income to God, you may feel like you are taking away from other necessities. Necessities like groceries, utilities, housing, all items you need to survive. Moreover, all those have major consequences if not paid. To help ease that fear, here is a prayer that Bishop Jakes offers to help you through this new challenge:

> Lord, heal me from the stress and the pressure that I get from worrying about my perception among my peers. Give me the gift of being satisfied by what you want me to have and when you know I can handle it. I thank you that you are teaching me to walk beside you and not in front of you. I repent for the times I got ahead of you. I regret the times you were trying to bless me and I was somewhere behind you, groveling with old issues. From this day forward I walk with you in peace and prosperity, knowing who I am, where I am and whose I am.

I am prepared to be blessed financially with the practical steps I am learning. But my focus is on you, for now I know that you are the greatest richness attainable and when I seek you first other things will happen as I prepare myself for what you have for me. Thank you for maturity coming to me spiritually, financially, and emotionally. My family will be blessed by what you are teaching me now. Amen.

# *Chapter Seven:*
# *Greed and Debt*

"A man is rich in proportion to the number of things which he can afford to leave alone"

-Henry David Thoreau

Greed is the insatiable desire to acquire more.  For some this desire runs out of control and leads to overwhelming debt.  The vicious circle is even more out of control in our day because of easy credit.  Overextended debt obligates you to someone other than God.  If you have to work overtime or even two jobs in order to extend your credit and acquire extras, you have obligated yourself to someone or something-your debt.  Your life is no longer yours.  You suffer, your family suffers and your relationship to God suffers.

Ask yourself why, ask yourself how.  Why am I in debt, how did I get in debt.  Some of the most common reasons are: failure to set goals, lack of information, too many fixed expenses, failure to plan emergencies, overestimate income, underestimate expenses, impulse buying, failure to communicate, failure to say no to kids, failure to keep records.  A rule of thumb to follow is your total debt minus your mortgage/rent should equal 10% for singles; 15% for those married and no children; and 20% plus three months of living expenses in saving for those married with children.

Luke 12:15 says, "Take care!  Be on your guard against all kinds of greed; for one's life does not consist in the abundance of possessions" (NRS).

So how do you tame your greed and get out of debt? TAKE CHARGE! Commit to getting spending **and** charging under control. From the last chapter, you should have a good framework for your budget. By reviewing your budget, you can see what needs to be trimmed or even eliminated. There are two steps to financial freedom: Step One, Identify your goals. One of your goals is having enough money to tithe. Step Two, Identify your resources, and credit should not be one of them! From these two steps, you can begin to change your spending habits. Some ways to do this would be: don't charge perishables; ask for cash discounts; don't buy on impulse. Check your motives when making a purchase. Ask yourself, do I **need** it? Learn to distinguish between your needs and your wants. Have I done my research (i.e. comparison shopped, looked it up in *Consumer Reports*)? Is the price reasonable? Is it really a sale price? Can I substitute something else for it? And the biggie; Will it solve my inner need? If you cannot answer yes to all those questions, then you should not make the purchase.

Here is a five-point plan to help begin to get your debt under control:

1. Control Plastic. If you cannot handle the temptation to overextend your credit, get rid of all your credit cards.
2. Understand the situation (your financial plan, budget, debt load).
3. Understand your goals (reasonable, obtainable).

4. Win the budget battle – "Do you have the money"?
5. Develop a plan to roll over debt (i.e. pay highest interest first, once paid, roll over payment to next highest interest or pay off the lowest balance first, once paid off, roll over payment to next lowest balance).

Once you have your debt under control you can begin to pay God (tithe) and yourself (savings)!

Bringing your debt under control will most likely be the hardest task you have undertaken.  So take a deep breath, pray about it, and then make the commitment and JUST DO IT!  Celebrate your accomplishments along the way and remember, "How can I soar like an eagle, when I keep spending like a turkey"?

In our next chapter we'll look at financial attitude.

# Chapter Eight:
# Financial Attitude

So far, you have begun your financial plan by creating and fine tuning your budget and working on getting your debt under control.  Now let's talk about attitude.  Financial attitude, that is.  Without the right financial attitude, all the work you've done so far and the work you'll continue to do will be just that – work!  And if it's work it's not fun which means you'll eventually abandon your financial planning for something that is fun.  Brooke Stephens, a financial analyst, commentator and author has this to say about financial attitude:

"How you manage your money is a reflection of how you manage your whole life.  Lazy, irresponsible, uneducated?  All those qualities can show up in how you handle your funds.  If you don't manage your money, credit card debt piles up; past due bills mount; and you live your life paycheck to paycheck. Instead of managing and enjoying your money, your money is managing you."

"But it doesn't have to be that way.  It all starts with attitude-the RIGHT attitude."

"Developing a money mentality requires thinking, planning and doing more than the required daily minimum effort to get a paycheck".

Her formula for a comfortable financial future:

- Get serious about financial habits, attitudes and choices.  Trying to buy recognition, esteem and respectability with material goods is a ridiculous waste of precious assets.

- Set up a financial plan and stick with it.  This is part of stewardship.  Stewardship is more than making offerings at church.  It also includes a financial portfolio and estate planning that allows you to have the greatest impact with what God has given you.
- Establish priorities that give you some financial control.
- Develop a daily or weekly routine that includes reading a financial periodical or tuning into a financial talk show.
- Think about what you're doing daily in terms of income and expenses.  For example, is doing the laundry creating income or expense?

Educate yourself.  Read books.  Find a financial mentor.  Seek information on handling money.  You can get ahead on your own if you make the effort to find out how to do it.

"I put money and sex in the same category" Stephen says.  "No one is going to tell you the right way to do either".

"Money management and financial planning may sound like intimidating terms that apply only to the rich, but if that's what you think, you're wrong.  If you earn a living, pay your bills on time, save for the future and invest in an IRA, you are practicing the first basic steps in the wealth-building process".

In the last chapter we look at savings so that the money we are saving begins to work for us instead of us working for it.

# Chapter Nine: The Final Point-Saving

By this time you should have a clear picture of where all your money is going by reviewing your monthly budget; on the way to reducing debt and use of credit; and even see the first signs of some extra cash at the end of the month with the financial planning you've been doing.  But with the extra income do you splurge and then it's gone again?  No.  You begin putting it away so that the money you are saving begins to work for you instead of you working for it.

Some helpful tips on saving are to:  Have automatic deposit of payroll checks with a predetermined amount going into saving first (aim for 10%, remember this is the concept of paying yourself second, remember to pay God first, and aren't you worth 10%), then the remainder going into checking for bill paying.  Or to deposit all refund reimbursements into savings.  Putting half of your tax refund into savings.  Split pay raises, bonuses; half for spending half into savings.  When installment loans are completed, keep paying only having the payment put into where... you got it – savings!

By putting the strategies you have learned so far to work for you, you will soon be able to start accomplishing the goals you originally set your sights on.  And remember, one of those goals was to have enough money to tithe. The hard, laborious work of budgeting and financial planning is now behind you.  The next task is to be faithful and committed to adhering to your budget and financial plan.  Like dieting, this can be the most daunting duty to maintain.  However, with prayerful encouragement from God, making new financial habits routine and diligent effort on your part, you shall see the fruits of your labor and start making those fruits labor for you!

In closing here is one last list for you to contemplate dealing with the 10 principles of financial independence.

1. Save consistently by living on less than you earn.
2. Study the investment methods and strategies of successful people and seek advice only from those who are competent through their own achievements to give it.
3. Learn to apply the principles of compounding, discounting and leveraging.
4. Never bet on a loser because you think its luck is about to change.
5. Think twice before investing in anything that eats. Those deals are much easier to get into than out of.
6. Don't invest in anything you can't explain to your spouse.
7. Reinvest all proceeds until financial independence is achieved.
8. Never get involved in anything that promises quick riches.  Trying to get rich quick is another form of gambling.  God says, "The plans of the diligent lead to profit as surely as haste leads to poverty" (Prov. 21:5, NIV).  If you try to get rich quickly, you'll get poor even quicker.

9. Be constantly on guard against every form of greed. No matter how much you have, wealth never brings lasting happiness. Wealth without God is death. See Luke 12:15-21.
10. Get started! A good plan today is better than a perfect plan tomorrow. Unless you were born wealthy, chances are you will have to sacrifice financially during part of your life. It is much better if that happens by choice when you are young than by force when you are too old to recover. The decision is yours.

# *In Closing*

It is my aspiration and intention that this book has given you the hope, desire and tools to bring your finances back under control and in line with God's financial management plan.  And that it will lead you towards a closer relationship with the Lord.

If you do not know Jesus as you personal Lord and Savior, please pray this prayer:

Lord Jesus, I am a sinner in need of a Savior. I believe that You are the Son of God and that You died on the cross, a living sacrifice for my sins. I surrender my life to You. Please forgive me for my sins and create in me a new heart oh Lord that desires to serve You all the days of my life. I accept You as my Lord and Savior. Amen.

# A Tithing Bibliography

Along my stewardship journey I have come across and relied upon several great resources that have made me a better steward and given me a deeper understanding of tithing.  I would like to share with you some of the resources that helped with the writing of this book.

**Hinze, Donald**. *To Give and Give Again.* Pilgrim Press, Cleveland, June 1990.

**Jackson, James.** *Whatcha Gonna Do With Whatcha Got.* Cook Communications Ministries Intl, Colorado Springs, May 1988.

**Jakes, Thomas D**. *The Great Investment.* G.P. Putnam's Sons, New York, 2000.

**Joiner, Don.** *Christians And Money: A Guide To Personal Finance.* Discipleship Resources, Nashville, April 1991.